FANTASIA ON

GREENSLEEVES

ADAPTED FROM THE OPERA

SIR JOHN IN LOVE

R. VAUGHAN WILLIAMS

ARRANGED FOR VIOLA OR VIOLONCELLO AND PIANOFORTE BY

WATSON FORBES

OXFORD UNIVERSITY PRESS

FANTASIA ON
GREENSLEEVES

Arranged for Viola (or Violoncello)
and Pianoforte by
WATSON FORBES

R. VAUGHAN WILLIAMS

Time of Performance 4 mins.

Copyright 1947 Oxford University Press

Printed in Great Britain

OXFORD UNIVERSITY PRESS, MUSIC DEPARTMENT, GREAT CLARENDON STREET, OXFORD OX2 6DP

3

Allegretto (♩ = ♩.)

p espressivo

fpp
una corda

sempre lontano

loco

p espressivo
staccato

*Folk Tune 'Lovely Joan'

4

VIOLONCELLO

FANTASIA ON
GREENSLEEVES

Arranged for Viola
and Pianoforte by
WATSON FORBES

R. VAUGHAN WILLIAMS

VIOLA

*The small notes may be omitted
Time of Performance 4 mins.

VIOLA

FANTASIA ON
GREENSLEEVES

Arranged for Violoncello
and Pianoforte by
WATSON FORBES

R. VAUGHAN WILLIAMS

VIOLONCELLO

Time of Performance 4 mins.

6

Reproduced and printed by
Halstan & Co. Ltd., Amersham, Bucks., England

7

OXFORD UNIVERSITY PRESS